BOBBY GALLAGHER

Busted vs McFly : Battle of the Bands

Copyright © 2024 by Bobby Gallagher

All rights reserved. No part of this publication may be reproduced, stored or transmitted in any form or by any means, electronic, mechanical, photocopying, recording, scanning, or otherwise without written permission from the publisher. It is illegal to copy this book, post it to a website, or distribute it by any other means without permission.

Bobby Gallagher asserts the moral right to be identified as the author of this work.

Bobby Gallagher has no responsibility for the persistence or accuracy of URLs for external or third-party Internet Websites referred to in this publication and does not guarantee that any content on such Websites is, or will remain, accurate or appropriate.

Designations used by companies to distinguish their products are often claimed as trademarks. All brand names and product names used in this book and on its cover are trade names, service marks, trademarks and registered trademarks of their respective owners. The publishers and the book are not associated with any product or vendor mentioned in this book. None of the companies referenced within the book have endorsed the book.

First edition

This book was professionally typeset on Reedsy. Find out more at reedsy.com

Contents

1	The Ultimate Showdown	1
2	Meet the Bands: Busted and McFly	7
3	Chart Wars: Who Topped the Charts?	14
4	Style Showdown: Music, Fashion, and Image	21
5	Live Performance Face-Off	28
6	Musical Mastery: Instruments and Skills	35
7	Fanbase Rivalry – Busted's Army vs. McFly's Galaxy Defenders	50
8	Memorable Collaborations and Crossover Moments	57
9	Behind the Scenes: Fun Facts, Trivia, and Easter Eggs	69
10	The Verdict: Who Reigns Supreme?	77
11	A Legacy of Two Legendary Bands	85

1

The Ultimate Showdown

P op your collar, dust off your air guitar, and get ready to "Crash the Wedding" and take a ride in the "Year 3000," because two of the UK's biggest pop-rock powerhouses, Busted and McFly, are about to go head-to-head in the ultimate "Band vs Band" showdown! It's not just nostalgia that's bringing these two iconic bands together—it's a battle of talent, energy, and, of course, a little friendly competition. After all, when it comes to who dominates the stage, **who says it can't be a "Star Girl" versus a "Sleeping With the Light On" situation?**

The upcoming joint world tour, featuring Busted and McFly, promises not just a musical extravaganza, but a celebration of two groups that shaped an entire generation's soundtrack. It's a tour that screams, "we grew up with these guys," but also raises the stakes as we ask: who reigns supreme? Don't be fooled by their playful rivalry—the stakes are real, and the fans are ready to cheer their favorite band to victory. So, let's dive into the backstory of this legendary tour and the epic face-off that will have fans screaming lyrics at the top of their lungs all around the world!

A Tale of Two Bands: Shaping the UK Pop-Rock Scene

To understand the gravity of this musical battle, we need to go back to the early 2000s when pop-punk was on the rise, and both Busted and McFly were at the top of the charts. The UK music scene was buzzing with energy, and these two bands played a massive role in shaping its sound. Their pop-rock anthems weren't just catchy; they were the soundtrack to an entire generation of teens navigating love, rebellion, and the occasional schoolboy crush.

Busted burst onto the scene in 2002 with their explosive debut, bringing a cheeky edge to the pop world with their power chords, punk attitude, and a flair for irreverence. Songs like "What I Go to School For" and "Crashed the Wedding" became instant hits, thanks to their rebellious, yet fun, themes. Busted had a knack for pairing tongue-in-cheek lyrics with energetic, anthemic music that made you want to jump around your room with your best mates. Their success was fast and furious, setting the bar for what a modern boy band could sound like—one that traded in choreography for guitars and attitude.

On the other hand, **McFly** came onto the scene in 2004, bringing with them a lighter, more polished sound, but with just as much energy and charisma. With their debut single "Five Colours in Her Hair," McFly established themselves as the poster boys of feel-good, sun-drenched pop-rock. They followed up with hits like "Obviously" and "All About You," blending catchy melodies, tight harmonies, and just enough cheeky charm to steal hearts and dominate the airwaves. McFly's music may have been more polished, but their skill with instruments and songwriting was undeniable. Their ability to blend pop hooks with a rock edge made them a household name and kept them riding high in the charts.

Both bands embodied different aspects of the UK pop-rock movement. **Busted** brought the edgy, rebellious sound, while **McFly** mastered the art of feel-good rock that made you want to sing along at the top of your lungs. Together, they created a yin and yang dynamic in the UK music scene. But now, as they prepare to go toe-to-toe on this tour, it's time to settle the score: which band truly rocked our world the hardest?

Band vs Band: The Friendly Rivalry

The **Band vs Band** theme of the upcoming world tour isn't just a gimmick—it's a fun, playful acknowledgment of the comparisons that have been made between Busted and McFly since their earliest days. And let's be honest, haven't we all asked ourselves at some point, "Am I more of a Busted or a McFly fan?" It's the musical equivalent of choosing between pizza or burgers—both are delicious, but which one is your ultimate go-to?

For years, fans have debated which band has the upper hand,

and now it seems the bands themselves are getting in on the action. This tour pits them against each other in the best way possible, with a healthy dose of **"Who's better at this? Who's better at that?"** It's like watching your two best friends playfully compete, knowing that deep down, there's nothing but love and respect between them—but someone still has to win, right?

The tour will feature both bands performing their greatest hits, as well as some joint numbers, giving fans a chance to see them side-by-side. It's not just about reliving the glory days of teen anthems; it's about celebrating how these two bands evolved, stayed relevant, and continued to create music that resonates. And in true competitive spirit, fans can expect to see some playful jabs and banter between the bands as they push each other to bring their A-game to the stage.

It's this spirit of **mild competitiveness** that makes the tour so exciting. Sure, it's not going to end in a full-blown rock-off (or will it?), but the tour's premise sets the stage for each band to showcase what makes them unique. Busted will undoubtedly bring their high-energy, punk-infused hits that make you want to pogo along, while McFly will charm audiences with their infectious melodies and polished stage presence. In the end, it's the fans who will decide the winner. Whether you're team **"Thunderbirds Are Go"** or rooting for the "**Room on the 3rd Floor**" boys, one thing's for sure: this tour is going to be **"All About You"**—the fans.

The Legacy of Busted and McFly: Still Flying High

As we fast-forward to today, the continued influence of Busted and McFly on the UK pop-rock scene is undeniable. Both bands have had their ups and downs, from breakups and reunions to side projects and personal growth, but through it all, they've remained beloved by fans. They've both evolved musically, showing that they're not just riding a wave of nostalgia but still have something to say in today's music landscape.

For **Busted**, their reunion brought a more mature sound while still keeping their signature edge. They've embraced the fact that their fans have grown up with them, and their newer music reflects that evolution. But don't worry—there's still plenty of cheeky, guitar-driven fun for old-school fans.

McFly, meanwhile, has been steadily releasing music that continues to showcase their knack for blending catchy pop with rock sensibilities. They've never shied away from experimenting, showing that they're not just stuck in the past. They've managed to maintain their boyish charm while maturing both personally and musically.

In the end, this tour is more than just a chance to relive the golden days of 2000s pop-rock; it's a celebration of two bands that continue to influence and inspire new generations of music lovers. Whether it's the electric energy of Busted or the infectious hooks of McFly, both bands have carved out legacies that extend far beyond their early chart-topping days.

Ready to Rock: Let the Showdown Begin

So, whether you're dusting off your old **McFly** T-shirt or gearing up to scream the lyrics to **"Year 3000"**, the **Band vs Band** tour promises to be an unforgettable journey. It's more than just a concert—it's a celebration of two incredible bands, a chance to relive your youth, and, yes, maybe decide once and for all which band will come out on top.

At the end of the day, we're all winners—because with **Busted** and **McFly** sharing the stage, you're guaranteed one thing: an epic, heart-pounding show full of all the hits you know and love. Buckle up, because this battle is about to get loud!

2

Meet the Bands: Busted and McFly

Before the battle begins, let's get to know the contenders in this epic showdown: **Busted** and **McFly**. These two bands have left an indelible mark on the UK pop-rock scene, and now they're taking the stage together for what promises to be a legendary tour. But to fully appreciate the significance of this "Band vs Band" face-off, we need to understand where each band came from, their rise to stardom, and the unique flavors they bring to the world of music. So, let's dive into the origin stories of **Busted** and **McFly**, break down their key members, and explore the sounds that made them household names.

Busted Overview: Punk, Pop, and Rebellion

Busted wasn't just a band—they were a movement. Formed in 2000, **Busted** burst onto the UK music scene at a time when boy bands were all about synchronized dance moves and matching outfits. But Busted was different—they swapped slick choreography for guitars, messy hair, and a sound that was unapologetically rebellious. Their brand of pop-punk was edgy, fun, and relatable, blending catchy pop melodies with the energetic pulse of punk rock. It was the perfect recipe for a generation of kids who wanted to break free from the conventional pop mold, and Busted delivered exactly that.

The original lineup of Busted consisted of three key members:

- **Charlie Simpson** – the tall, brooding guitarist with a voice as raw as his guitar riffs. Charlie brought a harder, rockier edge to the band, often standing out with his deeper, more emotive vocals.
- **Matt Willis** – the cheeky bassist with a knack for catchy hooks and a rebellious attitude. Matt's energetic performances and devil-may-care persona made him an instant fan favorite.
- **James Bourne** – the brains behind many of Busted's biggest hits, James was the songwriting powerhouse of the group, infusing their tracks with wit, humor, and a keen sense of what made a good pop-punk anthem.

Together, these three formed a perfect trio, each bringing their own unique flair to the band. And their chemistry was electric. In 2002, they released their self-titled debut album, which was packed with instant classics like "What I Go to School For," "Year 3000," and "Sleeping with the Light On." The album was a smash hit, reaching number 2 on the UK charts and catapulting the band into stardom. With their catchy hooks and irreverent lyrics, **Busted** quickly became the voice of a generation of teens who were looking for something a little more rebellious in their pop music.

Busted's success didn't stop there. Their second album, **"A Present for Everyone"** (2003), solidified their place in pop-punk history with even more hits like "Crashed the Wedding" and "Who's David?". The album's mix of punk attitude and radio-friendly melodies struck a chord with fans, and it wasn't long before Busted were selling out arenas and winning awards left, right, and center. They even managed to snag **two BRIT Awards** and countless other accolades during their initial run.

But what truly set Busted apart was their **signature sound**. Their music was a perfect blend of pop-punk energy and witty storytelling. Songs like "Year 3000" played with futuristic, offbeat lyrics, while tracks like "Sleeping with the Light On" explored more emotional territory. With loud, power-chord-driven guitars, fast tempos, and an undeniable sense of fun, Busted's music was tailor-made for anyone who wanted to turn up the volume and rebel—just a little.

Though Busted broke up in 2005 (sending fans into collective heartbreak), their impact was long-lasting. Their reunion in 2016 reignited the passion of old fans and introduced them to a new generation. And now, with this upcoming tour, Busted is ready to bring that same rebellious energy to the stage once again.

McFly Overview: Feel-Good Pop with a Rock Twist

While Busted was all about rebellion, **McFly** was all about charm. Formed in 2003, McFly brought a fresh, feel-good vibe to the UK music scene, blending upbeat pop melodies with just the right amount of rock edge. Named after Marty McFly from *Back to the Future*, the band had a retro-inspired style that made them stand out from the crowd. With their sun-soaked harmonies, catchy riffs, and infectious personalities, McFly quickly became a band you couldn't help but love.

McFly's lineup of four talented musicians has remained consistent since day one:

- **Tom Fletcher** – the band's primary songwriter and rhythm guitarist. Tom was the heart and soul of McFly's sound, penning most of their hits and bringing a sense of warmth and nostalgia to their music.
- **Danny Jones** – the band's lead guitarist and co-lead vocalist. Danny's powerful, raspy voice gave McFly's songs an edge, while his guitar skills added a rockier dimension to their music.
- **Dougie Poynter** – the cool and quirky bassist who brought personality to the band both on and off the stage. Dougie's playful attitude and solid basslines helped drive McFly's catchy sound.
- **Harry Judd** – the band's drummer and the backbone of their rhythm section. Harry's precision and energy behind the kit gave McFly's music its tight, polished feel.

McFly first exploded onto the scene in 2004 with their debut album, **"Room on the 3rd Floor"**, which featured the smash hit single "Five Colours in Her Hair." The song went straight to number one on the UK charts, and McFly became the youngest band to have their debut album hit the top spot. Their music was instantly recognizable for its upbeat, sunshiny vibe, blending rock guitars with bright pop melodies. Hits like "Obviously" and "That Girl" showcased McFly's knack for writing songs that were fun, relatable, and endlessly catchy.

What truly set McFly apart, though, was their ability to blend **pop and rock elements** so seamlessly. Their songs had the kind of sing-along choruses that were impossible to resist, but there was also real musical craftsmanship behind their sound. Whether it was Tom's heartfelt lyrics, Danny's powerful vocals, or the band's tight harmonies, McFly always delivered songs that made you feel good.

As their career progressed, McFly continued to release hit after hit, with standout albums like **"Wonderland"** (2005) and **"Motion in the Ocean"** (2006). Their feel-good anthems like "All About You" and "Star Girl" became staples in the UK music scene, earning them legions of devoted fans. Over the years, they've picked up numerous awards, including **a BRIT Award**, and cemented their status as one of the most beloved pop-rock bands in the UK.

Even as their music matured over time, McFly has always maintained that sense of fun and optimism that made them so appealing in the first place. Their ability to mix nostalgia with fresh, modern sounds has kept them relevant well into the 2020s, and their live performances remain a high-energy celebration of everything that makes McFly great.

Quick Comparison: Busted's Punk Edge vs McFly's Pop Charm

Now that we've met both bands, it's time for a quick comparison. On the surface, Busted and McFly seem like polar opposites, but their complementary styles are part of what makes their joint tour so exciting.

- **Busted** is all about edgy pop-punk with a rebellious attitude. Their three-member lineup (Charlie, Matt, and James) creates a more stripped-back, raw sound that's driven by power chords, punchy drums, and lyrics that range from humorous to heartfelt.
- **McFly**, on the other hand, brings a more polished, pop-rock vibe. Their four-member dynamic (Tom, Danny, Dougie, and Harry) allows for rich harmonies, intricate melodies, and a broader sound that feels uplifting and melodic.

In essence, **Busted** gives you that rebellious kick you need when you want to break the rules, while **McFly** provides the feel-good soundtrack for those sun-soaked days when everything just seems right. Both bands have left their own unique mark on the UK music scene, and together, they're about to take fans on the ride of a lifetime.

The **Busted vs McFly** showdown is more than just a battle of bands—it's a celebration of the diversity and brilliance of UK pop-rock. Whether you're into Busted's punky edge or McFly's irresistible charm, there's no denying that both bands have earned their place in music history. Now, the only question left is: which band will come out on top in this epic tour?

3

Chart Wars: Who Topped the Charts?

Get ready for a **chart showdown** like no other! In this corner, we have **Busted**, the kings of rebellious pop-punk anthems that made us dream of living in the "Year 3000." And in the opposite corner, there's **McFly**, the feel-good, harmony-driven pop-rockers with more "Five Colours in Her Hair" than we knew existed. This chapter dives into the numbers, the hits, and the bragging rights in this **Chart Wars** battle. So, who really topped the charts? Let's find out as we compare these two pop-rock giants, track by track, album by album.

Busted: Punk Pop Hits and Chart Domination

Busted didn't just crash the wedding—they crashed the **UK charts** in a major way, bringing their blend of punk-pop to the masses and making sure everyone knew exactly what they were going to school for. Their rise to fame was fast and furious, and with only a few albums in their discography, Busted managed to make a lasting impression that put them firmly in the **chart-topping hall of fame**.

Studio Albums & Notable Hits

- **"Busted"** (2002):
- Their self-titled debut album was a seismic event in the early 2000s. With hits like **"What I Go to School For," "Year 3000,"** and **"Sleeping with the Light On,"** Busted launched straight into the hearts of a generation. Their cheeky lyrics, fast-paced guitar riffs, and boy-next-door appeal were a winning formula.
- The album peaked at **#2** on the UK Albums Chart, cementing Busted as a major player in the pop-punk scene. The singles, particularly **"Year 3000,"** became anthems, with **"What I Go to School For"** and **"Sleeping with the Light On"** becoming staples in early 2000s playlists.

- **"A Present for Everyone"** (2003):
- Busted's follow-up album, **"A Present for Everyone,"** was exactly that—a gift of even more chart-busting tunes. This album included iconic tracks like **"Crashed the Wedding," "Air Hostess,"** and **"Who's David?"**, which all became instant classics.
- "A Present for Everyone" landed at **#2** on the UK Albums Chart once again, but this time it brought a string of **#1 singles**, including **"Crashed the Wedding"** and **"Who's**

David?". Their ability to keep the hits rolling meant that Busted's presence on the charts was undeniable.

Chart Statistics: Busted by the Numbers

- **Number of Studio Albums**: 4 (including their reunion releases)
- **Number of UK #1 Singles**: 4
- **Number of UK Top 10 Singles**: 8
- **Biggest Hit**: **"Year 3000"** – Peaked at **#2** and became one of their most recognizable tracks globally.

In total, Busted managed to score **four #1 singles**, all while maintaining a rebellious, punk-infused energy that set them apart from their peers. And while they were just shy of scoring a **#1 album** during their initial run, their consistent presence in the top 5 proved they were a force to be reckoned with.

McFly: Pop-Rock Perfection and Chart Supremacy

If Busted was the rebellious older sibling, **McFly** was the charming, feel-good younger brother who could sing, harmonize, and melt your heart with ease. When McFly arrived on the scene, they not only carried on Busted's momentum, they also **surpassed them** in some major chart metrics. With a more polished sound and a knack for writing infectious pop songs, McFly quickly became chart royalty.

Studio Albums & Notable Hits

- **"Room on the 3rd Floor"** (2004):
- McFly's debut album took the charts by storm. With their signature hit **"Five Colours in Her Hair"** leading the charge, the band became the youngest group to debut at **#1** on the UK Albums Chart. The album's catchy tracks, like **"Obviously"** and **"That Girl,"** were impossible to resist, and their charm was undeniable.

- **"Wonderland"** (2005):
- The second album, **"Wonderland,"** solidified McFly's reign over the charts. With a more mature sound but still packed with feel-good vibes, the album hit **#1** again, marking McFly's back-to-back chart-topping success. Songs like **"All About You"** and **"I'll Be OK"** became instant favorites, and **"All About You"** in particular remains one of McFly's most beloved tracks.

- **"Motion in the Ocean"** (2006):
- McFly continued their chart-topping streak with their third studio album, which produced hits like **"Star Girl"** and **"Please, Please."** The album peaked at **#6**, but the singles continued to dominate the airwaves, proving that McFly wasn't just a flash in the pan—they were here to stay.

Chart Statistics: McFly's Reign

- **Number of Studio Albums**: 6
- **Number of UK #1 Singles**: 7
- **Number of UK Top 10 Singles**: 18
- **Biggest Hit**: "**All About You**" – A UK #1 hit that became a massive anthem, even outside the UK.

McFly's impressive run includes **seven UK #1 singles**, making them one of the most successful British pop bands of their era. They also boast a whopping **18 Top 10 singles**, proving that their chart success wasn't just a one-time thing—it was consistent, album after album.

Head-to-Head: Chart-Topping Comparisons

So, how do these two bands stack up when we put their chart achievements side by side?

- **Number of #1 Singles**:
- **Busted**: 4
- **McFly**: 7
- McFly takes the lead here, with seven chart-topping singles compared to Busted's four. Tracks like **"All About You"** and **"Star Girl"** helped propel McFly to greater chart success, giving them a slight edge in the **#1 singles race**.

- **Number of Top 10 Singles**:

- **Busted**: 8
- **McFly**: 18
- In terms of Top 10 hits, McFly again has the advantage. With nearly **double the number** of Top 10 singles, McFly's ability to consistently churn out hits gave them an undeniable presence on the charts for years.

- **Number of #1 Albums**:
- **Busted**: 0 (though both their first two albums peaked at #2)
- **McFly**: 2 (both their first two albums hit #1)
- McFly also takes the cake in the **albums department**. Their debut and sophomore albums both went straight to **#1**, while Busted's albums just missed the top spot, peaking at **#2**. McFly's ability to take their albums to the top of the charts cemented their status as **chart kings**.

Award Wins and Industry Recognition

Both bands have racked up some impressive industry accolades along the way.

- **Busted**:
- **2 BRIT Awards** (Best British Breakthrough Act, Best Pop Act)
- **Multiple Smash Hits Awards** and other recognitions.
- **McFly**:
- **1 BRIT Award** (Best British Pop Act)
- **5 Smash Hits Awards**

- Multiple nominations and wins at the **Nickelodeon UK Kids' Choice Awards**.

In terms of awards, Busted edges out McFly with their two **BRIT Awards**—a major feat for any band. However, McFly's massive fanbase helped them sweep up a host of other honors, making it a **close race** in terms of industry recognition.

And the Winner of the Chart Wars Is...

If we're talking pure numbers, **McFly** comes out on top in this **Chart Wars** battle. With **more #1 singles**, **more Top 10 hits**, and **#1 albums** to their name, McFly undeniably dominated the UK charts during their heyday. However, Busted's influence and undeniable impact cannot be discounted. After all, without **Busted paving the way** with their punk-pop rebellion, McFly might not have had such an easy rise to the top.

But don't be too quick to declare McFly the ultimate victor—remember, this is only the beginning of the battle. The **Band vs Band** tour promises to be an all-out war, with both bands bringing their biggest hits and loudest anthems to the stage. So, whether you're a fan of **"Year 3000"** or **"Five Colours in Her Hair,"** one thing's for sure: this showdown is going to be **"All About You"** and the music that shaped an era.

Let the battle continue!

4

Style Showdown: Music, Fashion, and Image

Pop-punk vs. Pop-rock. Rebellious lyrics vs. Heartfelt storytelling. Grunge-pop vs. Surfer-chic.** In this epic Style Showdown, Busted and McFly don't just face off in the world of music—they're battling it out on the catwalk too. Whether you're rocking out to **"Year 3000"** in a band tee and ripped jeans, or serenading your crush with **"All About You"** in a smart jacket and Converse, these two bands have always been about more than just music. Their fashion, image, and musical styles helped define an era, creating looks that were as memorable as their chart-topping hits. So, let's dive into this **band vs band** showdown and see how Busted and McFly's styles stack up in the worlds of music, fashion, and image.

Music Style Comparison: Pop-Punk Meets Pop-Rock

When it comes to musical style, Busted and McFly bring two very different sounds to the table. But that's exactly what makes this **Style Showdown** so much fun—these bands may come from the same era, but their influences and aesthetics couldn't be more distinct.

Busted: The Pop-Punk Rebels

If you've ever found yourself pogoing to the sound of power chords and shouting lyrics about crashing weddings, there's a good chance **Busted** was your go-to band in the early 2000s. Busted burst onto the scene with a **pop-punk** sound that took its cues from American skate culture, bands like Blink-182, and a dash of British cheekiness for good measure. Their music had all the hallmarks of pop-punk: fast tempos, power chords, and that perfect mix of rebellion and playfulness that made teenagers everywhere want to grab a skateboard and skip school.

From their very first hit, **"What I Go to School For,"** Busted made it clear that they weren't here to follow the rules. Their lyrics were full of cheeky humor, adolescent angst, and just the right amount of rebellion. Whether it was fantasizing about time travel in **"Year 3000,"** causing chaos in **"Crashed the Wedding,"** or bemoaning the perils of teenage life in **"Sleeping with the Light On,"** Busted's music captured the **spirit of youth** in a way that was both rebellious and relatable.

Musically, Busted was defined by their **high-energy, guitar-**

driven sound. Their songs were filled with punchy rhythms, loud drums, and shout-along choruses that made you want to scream the lyrics at the top of your lungs. And while their sound evolved slightly over the years—particularly after their 2016 reunion—Busted's core remained firmly rooted in the world of pop-punk, a genre that never shies away from a little rebellion and a lot of fun.

McFly: The Retro-Rock Charmers

On the other side of the battlefield, **McFly** brought a more polished, retro-inspired pop-rock sound to the table. From the moment they hit the scene with **"Five Colours in Her Hair,"** McFly established themselves as the feel-good band of the early 2000s, blending catchy pop hooks with the kind of rock-and-roll swagger that made you want to dance as much as sing along.

McFly's music was heavily influenced by **1960s rock and roll**, with bands like The Beatles and The Beach Boys serving as clear inspirations. You could hear it in their upbeat rhythms, jangly guitars, and harmonized vocals that evoked a sense of nostalgia for a simpler, sunnier time. Songs like **"Obviously," "All About You,"** and **"Star Girl"** were bursting with infectious melodies and lyrics that tugged at your heartstrings while making you smile.

Lyrically, McFly leaned more into the world of **romantic story-telling**, crafting songs about young love, heartbreak, and the highs and lows of relationships. While Busted was all about mischief and mayhem, McFly's lyrics were more likely to make you swoon. **"All About You"** remains one of the band's most beloved tracks—a sweet, heartfelt love song that still makes fans tear up (or dream of their own fairytale romance).

In terms of sound, McFly embraced a **softer, more melodic approach** compared to Busted's punchy power chords. They were equally at home with ballads as they were with up-tempo hits, and their knack for songwriting was clear in their carefully crafted harmonies and intricate arrangements. McFly's music made you feel good—whether you were dancing to **"Five Colours in Her Hair"** or swaying along to **"The Heart Never Lies,"** their pop-rock charm was undeniable.

Fashion Battle: Grunge-Pop vs. Surfer-Chic

When it comes to fashion, Busted and McFly's styles were just as distinct as their music. Whether you were more into **grunge-pop rebellion** or **preppy surfer chic**, each band brought their own unique aesthetic to the stage—and to the wardrobes of fans everywhere.

Busted: Grunge-Pop Rebellion

From the very start, **Busted's fashion** screamed rebellion. While other boy bands were donning matching suits and perfect haircuts, Busted was rocking **ripped jeans, oversized t-shirts, and Converse sneakers** like they'd just rolled out of a skate park. Their look was heavily influenced by **grunge and skate culture**, taking cues from bands like Green Day and Sum 41. The message was clear: these guys were here to have fun, break some rules, and look cool doing it.

Each member of Busted brought his own twist to the band's overall aesthetic. **Charlie Simpson** leaned into the grunge side of things with his longer hair, dark clothes, and brooding looks. **Matt Willis** embraced the punk vibe with his spiky hair and leather jackets, while **James Bourne** went for a more casual, skater-boy look with graphic tees and hoodies.

Iconic fashion moments? Look no further than the **"Year 3000"** music video, where the guys donned futuristic gear that somehow still managed to look effortlessly cool, or the **"Crashed the Wedding"** video, where they took over a formal event in true Busted fashion—by causing chaos in ripped jeans and punk-rock style.

As the years went on, Busted's style evolved slightly, especially during their reunion era. They traded in some of the grunge for a more polished rock look—think leather jackets, skinny jeans, and boots. But no matter how their fashion evolved, the core of Busted's image remained rooted in that **grunge-pop rebellion** that made them stand out from the start.

McFly: Preppy Surfer Chic

On the flip side, **McFly's fashion** was all about clean-cut, preppy style with a hint of surfer cool. In their early days, the band often sported **striped polos, button-up shirts, and Converse sneakers**, with an easygoing, **California-inspired vibe** that made them look like they could have stepped straight off a surfboard. If Busted was the rebellious older sibling, McFly was the charming heartthrob you couldn't help but love.

Each member of McFly had his own fashion identity as well. **Tom Fletcher** often went for a classic, preppy look with cardigans and well-fitted shirts. **Danny Jones** leaned into a rock-inspired style with leather jackets and band tees, while **Dougie Poynter** embraced a quirkier, more laid-back surfer vibe with beanies, skinny jeans, and brightly colored tees. And let's not forget **Harry Judd**, who often rocked a more polished, sharp look, perfect for the dashing drummer of the group.

McFly's **most iconic fashion moment**? The music video for **"Five Colours in Her Hair"** is hard to beat. The guys donned bright, retro-inspired outfits that matched the song's playful energy, and the video became an instant classic, cementing their status as the ultimate feel-good band.

As McFly's music evolved, so did their style. In later years, the band traded in their polos for **more rock-inspired looks**, but they never lost that clean-cut charm that made them so lovable. Whether they were rocking leather jackets or classic denim, McFly's style was always effortlessly cool—and always left fans swooning.

Final Thoughts: Who Wins the Style Showdown?

So, who comes out on top in this **Style Showdown**? Well, that depends on your vibe.

- If you're all about **rebellion, ripped jeans, and skate culture**, then Busted's grunge-pop aesthetic is likely to win you over. Their style perfectly matched their music—loud, unapologetic, and always a little rough around the edges.
- But if you're more into **feel-good fashion, preppy looks, and surfer cool**, McFly's clean-cut style might just take the cake. Their polished, retro-inspired outfits made them the perfect heartthrobs for anyone who wanted a little sunshine with their rock.

Ultimately, the **Style Showdown** between Busted and McFly isn't just about who looked better—it's about how their **music and fashion intertwined** to create two iconic looks that defined a generation. Whether you were moshing to Busted in your Converse or dancing to McFly in your skinny jeans, both bands gave us something to aspire to.

And the best part? With this **Band vs Band** tour on the horizon, we get to relive both styles all over again—rebellion, charm, and all!

5

Live Performance Face-Off

Live Performance Face-Off

If there's one thing we know about Busted and McFly, it's that these bands know how to **put on a show**. Whether it's Busted crashing into your ears with their punk-infused energy or McFly serenading the crowd with their pop-rock charm, both bands bring something special to the stage. But in the spirit of this **Band vs Band** tour, the question remains: **who's got the better live show?** Is it the chaotic fun of Busted, or the polished perfection of McFly? Let's break it down and dive into the ultimate **live performance face-off** between two of the UK's most beloved bands.

Busted's Concert Energy: Chaos, Fun, and Pure Punk Attitude

When it comes to live performances, **Busted** doesn't just play their songs—they bring the house down with an explosion of **high-energy chaos**. Their concerts are more like **punk-pop parties**, where the stage becomes a playground for the band to bounce around, interact with the crowd, and deliver their hits with reckless abandon. From the moment they step on stage, Busted's attitude is clear: they're here to have fun, break a few rules, and make sure the audience does too.

Youthful Punk Attitude

From their early days, Busted built a reputation for being **unpredictable on stage**, and that's what fans loved about them. You never knew what to expect—whether it was **Matt Willis** jumping off an amp mid-song, **Charlie Simpson** shredding a guitar solo while running across the stage, or **James Bourne** cracking jokes with the crowd between songs, Busted always kept the energy level at 11.

Their concerts are the epitome of **youthful rebellion**, with fans screaming along to anthems like **"What I Go to School For"** and **"Crashed the Wedding."** There's a sense of camaraderie between the band and the audience, as if Busted is inviting the entire crowd to join in on the mayhem. Whether they're leaping into the air during **"Year 3000"** or whipping the crowd into a frenzy with the punky beats of **"Air Hostess,"** Busted's performances are packed with adrenaline, creating a contagious sense of excitement that makes you want to throw yourself into the mix.

Chaotic Fun

Busted's concerts are nothing if not **chaotically fun**. The band thrives on spontaneity, with impromptu crowd singalongs and unexpected antics making every performance feel unique. Their punk-pop sound is perfectly suited for live shows, with fast tempos, crunchy guitars, and loud drums that get the audience jumping up and down. It's not just a concert—it's an experience.

One of the best things about Busted's live shows is the way they never take themselves too seriously. Even in the middle of a heart-pounding set, the band always finds time for a bit of playful banter or a cheeky joke. Whether they're poking fun at each other on stage or pulling a fan on stage to join in, Busted's performances are full of **laughs, mischief, and pure, unfiltered joy.**

Memorable tour moments? How about the time Matt Willis **stage-dove** into the crowd at a 2003 gig, or the moment Charlie Simpson decided to cover Blink-182's **"All the Small Things"** mid-set, sending the audience into a nostalgic frenzy? Busted's live performances are full of these off-the-cuff moments that make every show feel like a one-of-a-kind experience.

McFly's Stage Presence: Polished Perfection with Humor and Heart

While Busted might lean into chaos, **McFly** brings a different kind of energy to their live shows—one that's all about **polished performances, musical skill, and a whole lot of charm**. McFly's concerts are tight, well-rehearsed, and full of the kind of showmanship that leaves you in awe of their talent. But don't be fooled by the polish—McFly knows how to keep things fun, and their ability to balance humor, heart, and musicality makes them stand out as live performers.

Polished Performances

From the very beginning, McFly has always been about **delivering a top-notch performance**. Their shows are known for being **musically tight**, with each member showing off their instrumental prowess while still keeping things light and playful. Whether it's **Tom Fletcher** delivering a flawless guitar solo or **Harry Judd** banging out a drumbeat with the precision of a metronome, McFly's live performances are a masterclass in musical skill.

Their ability to **switch between upbeat, high-energy tracks** like **"Five Colours in Her Hair"** and heartfelt ballads like **"The Heart Never Lies"** shows just how versatile they are as performers. One minute they're making you jump up and down, and the next they've got the entire crowd waving their arms and singing along to a soulful tune. Their setlists are designed to take the audience on a journey, blending the band's infectious pop-rock hits with moments of emotional depth that leave you feeling all the feels.

Humor and Crowd Interaction

If there's one thing McFly excels at, it's their ability to **connect with the crowd**. Their concerts feel like an intimate gathering of friends, even when they're playing to packed arenas. **Tom, Danny, Dougie, and Harry** are constantly cracking jokes, sharing stories, and making the audience feel like they're part of the show. Their natural banter and laid-back charm make them incredibly relatable, and it's not uncommon to see Tom or Danny poking fun at each other mid-song or getting the crowd involved in some ridiculous on-stage game.

One of McFly's most **memorable tour moments** was during their **"Wonderland Tour"** when they introduced a game called **"Danny vs. Dougie,"** where the two would compete in bizarre challenges like who could eat a banana the fastest. It was moments like these that made McFly shows not just concerts, but events filled with laughter and fun.

Their fans also play a big role in making the shows special. McFly is known for getting the audience involved, whether it's by asking them to sing a chorus, inviting them to clap along to the beat, or even letting fans choose the next song. There's a sense of **mutual admiration** between McFly and their fans that elevates their live performances into something truly memorable.

Who's Got the Better Show?

So, who wins the **Live Performance Face-Off**? Let's take a closer look at what each band brings to the table:

- **Busted's Strengths**:
- **Energy**: Busted's punk-infused performances are packed with high-energy antics that get the crowd buzzing from start to finish.
- **Spontaneity**: You never know what to expect at a Busted show, and that unpredictability adds an exciting edge to their live performances.
- **Fun**: With their playful banter and chaotic on-stage antics, Busted always makes sure their concerts are as fun for the audience as they are for the band.

- **McFly's Strengths**:
- **Polish**: McFly's performances are polished to perfection, with each note hitting the mark and each song delivered with finesse.
- **Humor and Heart**: McFly's ability to balance laugh-out-loud moments with heartfelt songs makes their concerts a rollercoaster of emotions in the best possible way.
- **Crowd Interaction**: No band connects with their fans quite like McFly, and their shows often feel like a big family gathering.

The truth is, it's hard to declare a clear winner when both bands bring such **different vibes** to the stage. If you're looking for a

chaotic, adrenaline-pumping show that feels like a punk-pop party, Busted might edge out McFly. But if you prefer a **polished, emotionally engaging performance** that mixes humor with heartfelt tunes, McFly might take the crown.

What to Expect from the Joint Tour: Band vs Band

With the **Band vs Band** tour on the horizon, fans are in for a real treat. Imagine the **chaos of a Busted show** combined with the **polish of a McFly concert**, all in one night. The tour promises to be a **musical battle** of epic proportions, with each band pushing the other to new heights. Will Busted's **youthful punk energy** outshine McFly's **crowd-pleasing charm**? Or will McFly's **musical tightness and humor** win over the audience?

Fans can expect a night of **back-and-forth banter**, **hit after hit**, and plenty of **surprises** along the way. And who knows— maybe there'll even be some on-stage challenges to keep the competition going!

One thing's for sure: whether you're team Busted or team McFly, this tour is going to be an unforgettable experience that showcases the best of both worlds. So grab your air guitar, warm up your vocal cords, and get ready for a live show that's bound to go down in **pop-rock history**!

Let the showdown begin

6

Musical Mastery: Instruments and Skills

When it comes to **musical mastery**, both Busted and McFly know how to turn up the volume and rock out with the best of them. While their styles might differ—Busted brings the punk-pop punch, and McFly delivers polished pop-rock charm—both bands are packed with talented musicians who know their way around a stage and an instrument. In this chapter, we're diving deep into the **instrumental breakdown** of each band, taking a closer look at what makes their music so irresistible. Get ready for power chords, killer harmonies, and some serious **"Star Girl"** solos as we explore how these two pop-rock titans craft their sound.

Busted's Approach: Power Chords, Driving Rhythms, and Upbeat Tempos

If you've ever cranked up a Busted track like **"Crashed the Wedding"** or **"Year 3000"** and immediately felt the urge to start air-guitaring in your room, you're not alone. Busted's music is built on the foundations of **punk-pop energy**, with a focus on catchy melodies, driving rhythms, and upbeat tempos that get your heart racing. The band's approach to their instruments is all about raw power and fun—a **straightforward, no-nonsense rock attitude** that's perfectly suited for the live stage.

Guitars: Power Chords and Punchy Riffs

At the heart of Busted's sound is the **guitar**—and not just any guitar, but **power chords galore**. From the very first chords of **"What I Go to School For,"** you can feel the raw energy Busted brings to their music. **James Bourne** and **Charlie Simpson** are the guitar heroes of the band, and they make sure every song is packed with infectious riffs that are easy to play but impossible to forget.

Power chords are Busted's bread and butter—simple, fast, and designed to get you moving. Whether it's the catchy opening riff of **"Air Hostess"** or the crunchy guitars in **"Thunderbirds Are Go,"** Busted's approach to guitar is all about creating a sound that hits you in the chest and gets your adrenaline pumping. It's this simplicity, combined with their high-octane energy, that makes their music so addictive.

Charlie, in particular, brings a **heavier, rockier edge** to Busted's guitar work. His deep, growly vocals complement his guitar style, and he's not afraid to throw in the occasional guitar solo or heavier riff, especially during live performances. James, on the other hand, is more about those signature catchy hooks that make Busted songs instantly recognizable. Together, their guitars create a dynamic that balances punk-rock aggression with pop-friendly melodies.

Bass: The Backbone of the Band

Behind every great guitar riff is a solid bassline, and in Busted, **Matt Willis** holds it all down with his driving, rhythmic bass. Matt's basslines aren't flashy, but they're essential to the band's sound, adding depth and groove to each track. In songs like **"Sleeping with the Light On,"** the bass plays a crucial role in anchoring the song's more melodic moments, while in faster tracks like **"Dawson's Geek,"** the bass adds a relentless pulse that keeps the song charging forward.

What makes Matt's bass work stand out is its ability to be both **melodic and rhythmic**, seamlessly blending with the drums to create that punchy, up-tempo rhythm that defines Busted's sound. His energetic stage presence only adds to the excitement—he's often bouncing around the stage, making sure the bass never gets lost in the mix.

Drums: Fast, Furious, and Fun

No punk-pop band would be complete without a drummer who can keep up with the fast-paced energy, and Busted's drums are all about that **fist-pumping, head-banging attitude**. Their drummers, both in studio and live, lay down fast beats that drive their songs forward at breakneck speed. Songs like **"3AM"** and **"That Thing You Do"** are great examples of how Busted's drums create an upbeat, danceable rhythm that gives the band its signature youthful energy.

The drumming in Busted's music isn't about complex patterns—it's about **keeping the energy high** and the momentum going. Fast tempos, driving rhythms, and snappy fills are the order of the day, and they're a key ingredient in making Busted's live shows feel like an adrenaline-fueled rollercoaster ride.

McFly's Approach: Complex Arrangements, Harmonies, and Instrumental Versatility

While Busted thrives on straightforward, high-energy punk-pop, **McFly** takes a more **musically intricate approach**. Their songs are full of rich harmonies, clever arrangements, and instrumental versatility that show off their musical chops. If Busted is all about kicking down the door, McFly is about crafting a perfect pop-rock hit that sticks with you long after the last note fades.

Guitars: Melodic and Versatile

In McFly, the guitars are just as important as they are in Busted, but they take a different approach. **Tom Fletcher** and **Danny Jones** share guitar duties, and their playing styles complement each other perfectly. While Tom often handles rhythm guitar, keeping the songs grounded with **bright, jangly chords**, Danny steps in with lead guitar parts that add a bit of rock-and-roll flair. Together, their guitars create a layered sound that's both catchy and complex.

Take a song like **"Obviously"**—the guitars are upbeat and playful, with a rhythm that's easy to tap your foot to, while the lead guitar adds a touch of twang that gives the song its lighthearted, feel-good vibe. Then there's **"Room on the 3rd Floor,"** where Tom and Danny's guitars blend seamlessly with the vocals to create a sense of warmth and nostalgia. McFly's guitars are always melodic, but they never shy away from a good rock riff when the time calls for it—just listen to the punchy guitar in **"One for the Radio"** to see how McFly can rock out when they want to.

Bass: Melody Meets Groove

In McFly, the bass isn't just there to support the rhythm—it's an essential part of the **melodic structure**. **Dougie Poynter** is a talented bassist who knows how to make his instrument sing, often adding melodic flourishes that give McFly's music extra depth. In songs like **"Transylvania,"** Dougie's bassline isn't just following the chords—it's dancing around them, adding a layer of groove that makes the song stand out.

What makes Dougie's bass playing so effective is his ability to find the **balance between rhythm and melody**. He can lay down a solid foundation for the rest of the band, but he's not afraid to step out and add some flair when the moment calls for it. It's this attention to detail that gives McFly's music its richness, making each song feel more layered and complete.

Drums: Precision and Power

Harry Judd, McFly's drummer, is the unsung hero of the band's sound. Known for his **precision and power**, Harry's drumming is a perfect mix of technical skill and rock energy. He's just as comfortable laying down a steady beat for a ballad like **"All About You"** as he is driving the band through an up-tempo rocker like **"Five Colours in Her Hair."**

One of Harry's strengths is his ability to play with restraint when needed, letting the melody and vocals take center stage, but he knows when to turn up the intensity, too. His fills are always spot-on, and his dynamic control gives McFly's songs their emotional impact, whether he's gently tapping the snare in a softer section or bringing the house down with a crash of cymbals.

Harmonies: The Secret Ingredient

One of McFly's standout features is their **tight vocal harmonies**, which add a level of polish and professionalism to their music. The vocal blend between **Tom, Danny, and Dougie** is a big part of what makes McFly's sound so distinct. Songs like **"Star Girl"** and **"Love Is Easy"** are elevated by the harmonies that lift the choruses and make them soar. McFly's ability to seamlessly weave harmonies into their arrangements sets them apart from many other bands in the pop-rock genre, giving their songs a **rich, full sound** that's impossible to ignore.

Final Thoughts: Who Wins the Musical Mastery Face-Off?

So, who takes home the title of **musical mastery** in this **Band vs Band** showdown? It really depends on what you're looking for. **Busted** brings a raw, energetic punk-pop sound that's all about power chords, driving rhythms, and sheer fun. Their music is straightforward but packed with enough energy to make any crowd go wild. On the other hand, **McFly** offers a more polished, intricate approach, with complex arrangements, melodic basslines, and harmonies that add depth and emotion to their music.

If you're after **high-energy, no-frills punk-pop**, Busted's the band for you. But if you love **well-crafted pop-rock with a dash of musical flair**, McFly's your go-to. Both bands have mastered their respective styles, making this one of the most exciting musical face-offs in pop-rock history. One thing's for sure: whether it's Busted's punchy guitars or McFly's harmonized perfection, these two bands have got the musical chops to keep you rocking for years to come!

Members' Musical Talents

In the **Band vs Band** showdown, it's not just about the songs—it's about the musicians behind the music. Each member of Busted and McFly brings their own unique talents to the table, contributing to the success and signature sound of their respective bands. But let's be honest: we've all wondered at some point, **who's the stronger songwriter? Who's the true guitar hero?** And when it comes to bass and drums, which band's rhythm section reigns supreme?

In this chapter, we're diving deep into a friendly face-off between the band members themselves, comparing their musical talents and seeing how they stack up. From **James Bourne and Tom Fletcher's songwriting prowess** to a **bass showdown** between **Matt Willis and Dougie Poynter**, this is where we find out which band's members come out on top!

James Bourne vs. Tom Fletcher: Who's the Stronger Songwriter?

If there's one thing both **Busted** and **McFly** have in common, it's the sheer number of **catchy, memorable songs** they've written. And when it comes to the brains behind those hits, **James Bourne** of Busted and **Tom Fletcher** of McFly are the creative powerhouses driving their bands forward. But who's the stronger songwriter? Let's break it down.

James Bourne: The Punk-Pop Hitmaker

James Bourne has been at the heart of **Busted's songwriting** since day one. With his knack for catchy hooks, cheeky lyrics, and energetic melodies, James has crafted some of the most iconic punk-pop anthems of the early 2000s. From the rebellious charm of **"What I Go to School For"** to the futuristic fantasy of **"Year 3000,"** James's songwriting is all about capturing the spirit of youth in a way that's fun, humorous, and always a little mischievous.

What makes James stand out is his ability to write **universal,**

relatable songs that still feel fresh and exciting. His lyrics often tell stories that fans can connect with, whether it's dreaming about a high school crush or imagining life in a far-off future. And let's not forget his role in the **McBusted supergroup**, where his songwriting chops helped merge the best of both worlds.

Tom Fletcher: The Heartfelt Hitmaker

On the other side of the battle, **Tom Fletcher** is McFly's **songwriting mastermind**. With an impressive catalog of hits that includes **"All About You," "Five Colours in Her Hair,"** and **"Love Is Easy,"** Tom has proven himself as a songwriter who can blend heartfelt emotion with pop-rock charm. His songs are often characterized by their **melodic beauty** and **feel-good vibes**, making them perfect sing-along anthems for fans of all ages.

Tom's songwriting stands out for its **emotional depth**. He's just as comfortable writing fun, upbeat tracks as he is penning heartfelt ballads that tug at the heartstrings. Songs like **"The Heart Never Lies"** and **"Love Is on the Radio"** showcase his ability to craft lyrics that resonate with listeners on a personal level.

The Verdict:

While both James and Tom are incredibly talented songwriters, their strengths lie in different areas. James is the master of crafting **energetic, fun-filled anthems** that are all about youth, rebellion, and having a good time, while Tom's gift lies in his ability to write **emotionally rich, feel-good songs** that connect with fans on a deeper level. It's hard to pick a winner here because they both excel in their own lanes—but if you're looking for raw punk-pop energy, **James Bourne** has the edge, while **Tom Fletcher** takes the crown for heartfelt, melodic pop-rock.

Danny Jones vs. Charlie Simpson: Who's the Guitar Hero?

When it comes to shredding on stage and delivering unforgettable guitar riffs, **Danny Jones** of McFly and **Charlie Simpson** of Busted are the two contenders in this epic guitar battle. Both have carved out their own distinctive guitar styles, but who's the ultimate guitar hero?

Charlie Simpson: The Rocker with a Hard Edge

Charlie Simpson is known for bringing a **harder, rockier edge** to Busted's music. His deep, gravelly vocals complement his guitar playing, which often veers into **heavier, more aggressive territory** compared to the band's pop-punk foundation. Charlie's guitar work is packed with power chords, crunchy riffs, and a bit of grit, adding a **punk-rock intensity** to songs like **"Crashed the Wedding"** and **"Thunderbirds Are Go."**

But Charlie's talents don't stop there. After Busted's initial split, he went on to pursue a **solo career** with a much more introspective, alternative rock sound. This shift showcased his versatility as a guitarist, proving that he could handle everything from fast, punky riffs to more nuanced, atmospheric guitar lines.

Danny Jones: The Versatile Virtuoso

Danny Jones is McFly's guitar wizard, known for his **versatility and musicality**. Whether he's laying down the catchy, up-tempo riffs in **"Five Colours in Her Hair"** or delivering a bluesy, soulful solo in **"That Girl,"** Danny's guitar work is always on point. His playing style is heavily influenced by classic rock and roll, with a touch of blues, which gives McFly's music a more retro, throwback feel compared to Busted's punkier sound.

Danny's ability to seamlessly switch between **rhythm and lead guitar** adds an extra layer of complexity to McFly's music. He's just as comfortable cranking out a power chord as he is fingerpicking a delicate melody, and his solos are always a highlight of McFly's live shows.

The Verdict:

When it comes to pure rock intensity, **Charlie Simpson** brings a heavier, grittier edge to the guitar that's perfect for Busted's punk-pop anthems. But for **versatility and technical skill**, **Danny Jones** takes the title of guitar hero. His ability to blend rock, blues, and pop into his playing makes him a more well-rounded guitarist, giving McFly an extra layer of musical depth.

Dougie Poynter vs. Matt Willis: Bass Showdown

The **bass** may not always take the spotlight, but it's the backbone of every great band. In this showdown, we've got **Dougie Poynter** of McFly going up against **Matt Willis** of Busted in a battle of the basslines. Who's got the better groove?

Matt Willis: The Punk Bass Master

Matt Willis brings a no-nonsense, punk-inspired bass style to Busted. His basslines are fast, rhythmic, and designed to keep the momentum going. Matt's playing is all about **driving the song forward**, making sure the energy never dips, especially in Busted's more up-tempo tracks like **"Air Hostess"** and **"What I Go to School For."**

Matt's style is simple but effective—he lays down the foundation and keeps things tight, letting the guitars and vocals take the spotlight. But his bass playing is essential to the overall sound of Busted, adding that punchy, rhythmic backbone that keeps their songs feeling urgent and energetic.

Dougie Poynter: The Melodic Bassist

Dougie Poynter brings a different flavor to McFly's music. His basslines are often more **melodic**, weaving in and out of the guitar and vocal lines to create a richer, fuller sound. In songs like **"Transylvania"** and **"One for the Radio,"** Dougie's basslines aren't just supporting the rhythm—they're adding a melodic layer that gives the songs extra depth.

Dougie's bass playing is more complex than Matt's, but it's never flashy for the sake of being flashy. He knows how to find the perfect balance between melody and rhythm, making his basslines integral to McFly's overall sound.

The Verdict:

This one's a close call, but when it comes to pure **melodic mastery**, **Dougie Poynter** edges out **Matt Willis**. While Matt's basslines are all about driving the energy and keeping the beat, Dougie's more intricate, melodic approach adds an extra dimension to McFly's music.

Harry Judd: The Best Drummer Across Both Bands?

Now, let's talk about the backbone of any band—the drummer. In this case, **Harry Judd** of McFly stands out as the rhythmic force that keeps everything together. But is he the best drummer across both bands?

Harry Judd: The Precision Powerhouse

When it comes to drumming, **Harry Judd** is the definition of precision and power. His drumming is tight, dynamic, and always in perfect sync with the rest of the band. Whether he's laying down the solid beat of **"Obviously"** or bringing the energy up in **"Five Colours in Her Hair,"** Harry's drumming is all about **consistency and control**.

But Harry isn't just a timekeeper—he knows how to add **flair** when needed. His fills are always well-timed, and his ability to shift from soft, subtle drumming to full-blown rock anthems gives McFly's music an extra kick.

The Verdict:

Without a doubt, **Harry Judd** is the standout drummer across both bands. His technical skill, precision, and ability to enhance McFly's sound with his drumming make him a key part of the band's success. Plus, his stage presence and tight live performances cement his status as the rhythmic champion in this Band vs Band battle.

Final Thoughts: The Ultimate Musical Face-Off

In the end, the **musical mastery** of Busted and McFly comes down to their unique strengths:

- **James Bourne** and **Tom Fletcher** are both phenomenal songwriters, with James bringing the punk-pop energy and Tom delivering emotional, melodic pop-rock hits.
- **Charlie Simpson** and **Danny Jones** are both guitar heroes in their own right, with Charlie's rock intensity matched by Danny's versatile, technical playing.
- On bass, **Dougie Poynter's melodic flair** gives McFly an edge, while **Matt Willis's punk drive** powers Busted's high-energy sound.
- And finally, **Harry Judd's drumming** stands out as the

backbone that ties McFly's music together.

In this friendly face-off, it's clear that both bands are packed with talent, each member bringing their own unique skills to the table. So whether you're rocking out with Busted or singing along with McFly, you're in for a musical experience that's second to none!

7

Fanbase Rivalry – Busted's Army vs. McFly's Galaxy Defenders

Forget the battle of guitars and power chords—when it comes to Busted and McFly, some of the fiercest competition happens off-stage, in the hearts and minds of their **dedicated fanbases**. On one side, we have **Busted's Army**, a loyal brigade of pop-punk fans who stuck by the band through thick and thin, from their rebellious early years to their triumphant reunions. On the other side, there's **McFly's Galaxy Defenders**, a group of super-dedicated fans whose unwavering support has propelled McFly to pop-rock stardom for nearly two decades.

In this chapter, we're diving into the **fanbase rivalry** that has fueled the flames of Busted vs. McFly for years. From fan-driven campaigns and social media hype to those unforgettable moments where the fans became part of the show, we'll take a closer look at the **army and the defenders** and see which group might just have the upper hand in the ultimate fan showdown.

Busted's Fanbase: A Loyal Army of Pop-Punk Rebels

When Busted first hit the scene in 2002, they brought with them not just a string of catchy hits but a wave of fans who couldn't get enough of their cheeky lyrics, rebellious attitude, and pop-punk anthems. Known affectionately as **Busted's Army**, these fans weren't just casual listeners—they were die-hard supporters who lived and breathed everything Busted. Even when the band went on hiatus in 2005 (causing **thousands of hearts to break**), their fans kept the faith alive, hoping for the day their favorite trio would reunite and rock the world once more.

Demographics, Dedication, and Notable Moments

Busted's fanbase, much like their music, was built on the spirit of **youthful rebellion**. Their early fans were predominantly teenagers—students who could relate to the angst and excitement in songs like **"What I Go to School For"** and **"Sleeping with the Light On."** These fans weren't just looking for another boy band; they wanted a band that spoke to their experiences, frustrations, and dreams, all wrapped up in punk-pop energy. And Busted delivered that in spades.

As the years went on, those same fans stuck by Busted, even after the band split up. They **clung to the nostalgia** of the early 2000s, replaying classics like **"Year 3000"** and **"Crashed the Wedding,"** and patiently waiting for the band's return. And when Busted finally reunited in 2016, the fanbase came roaring back into action, proving that time hadn't dulled their dedication one bit.

One of the most notable moments for **Busted's Army** was their

reunion tour. Fans who had grown up with the band rushed to buy tickets, selling out venues and proving that Busted's music had stood the test of time. Fans flooded social media with stories about how much the band had meant to them, creating a sense of community and nostalgia that only the most dedicated fanbases can achieve.

Fan-Driven Campaigns and Milestones

Busted fans have always been vocal, but they really showed their power during the years of the band's hiatus. In an effort to bring their beloved band back, fans launched countless **online campaigns**, petitions, and social media movements to urge the members to reunite. Whether it was **#BringBackBusted** hashtags or heartfelt YouTube tribute videos, Busted's Army never gave up hope. And when the band finally announced their reunion, the fans could claim victory—they had helped make it happen.

But it wasn't just about getting Busted back together. Fans also played a massive role in supporting the band's newer music. Their 2016 album **"Night Driver"** was met with enthusiasm from long-time fans who were eager to see how the band had evolved. Social media was flooded with posts, memes, and videos of fans celebrating their return, sharing their excitement with the world and proving that they hadn't just been waiting—they had been **building anticipation** for years.

McFly's Fanbase: The Galaxy Defenders Strike Back

If Busted's Army was built on youthful rebellion, then **McFly's Galaxy Defenders** were all about pure, **heartfelt loyalty**. From the moment McFly burst onto the scene in 2004 with **"Five Colours in Her Hair,"** their fans were hooked—not just by the catchy melodies but by the band's charm, humor, and the deep connection they forged with their listeners. Known as the **Galaxy Defenders** (after the lyric in "Star Girl"), McFly's fans quickly became some of the most dedicated in the pop-rock world, showing up in droves to support the band through every new album, tour, and milestone.

McFly's Loyal Fans and Their Role in the Band's Success

McFly's success has always been tightly linked to their relationship with their fans. While their music was packed with infectious hooks and sing-along choruses, it was the **interaction with their fanbase** that made McFly stand out from other bands of the era. From the start, McFly made it clear that their fans were a part of the journey, often referring to them as an extended family.

This loyalty wasn't a one-way street—McFly went above and beyond to connect with their fans, from spontaneous meet-and-greets to interacting with fans on **social media**. Whether they were sharing behind-the-scenes moments on Twitter or getting fans involved in choosing setlists for their tours, McFly knew how to keep their fans feeling **valued and appreciated**.

One of the most iconic fan moments came during McFly's

"Wonderland Tour," where they played a game called **"Danny vs. Dougie"** live on stage, with fans voting in real-time to decide the outcome of silly challenges. It was the perfect example of how McFly's concerts weren't just about music—they were about creating memories and **engaging directly with the audience**.

Notable Fan Moments and Interaction with the Band

McFly has always been generous with their time, often surprising fans with **exclusive events** or hanging out with them after shows. One of the most notable moments came during their **"Above the Noise" Tour**, when fans created a massive project to thank the band for their years of music. Thousands of fans participated in the "**Thank You McFly**" campaign, flooding the band's social media with messages of gratitude, sharing photos, and organizing tributes. The campaign left McFly visibly moved, and they dedicated songs during the tour to their incredible fanbase.

McFly also engaged with their fans through their **SuperCity website**, a platform that gave fans exclusive access to content, including behind-the-scenes videos, early song releases, and even live chats with the band. This deep connection helped build a **community of loyal fans** who weren't just there for the music—they were there for the shared experience of being a McFly fan.

Whose Fans Are More Hardcore?

So, who wins the **ultimate fanbase rivalry**—Busted's Army or McFly's Galaxy Defenders? Let's break it down.

Fan Dedication

Both fanbases are incredibly dedicated, but their approaches differ. **Busted's Army** went through the heartbreak of a long hiatus, but their loyalty never wavered. The online campaigns, petitions, and social media buzz they generated during those years without the band were impressive, to say the least. When Busted finally reunited, it felt like a victory not just for the band but for the fans who had kept the dream alive.

On the other hand, **McFly's Galaxy Defenders** have been there from day one, showing consistent support for the band through every album, tour, and evolution of their sound. Their loyalty isn't just about nostalgia—it's about being there through the highs and lows, whether it's cheering on the band's romantic ballads or rocking out to their pop-punk hits.

Social Media Presence

In the age of social media, both fanbases have dominated online spaces. **Busted's Army** has organized some of the most impressive online campaigns, from reunion demands to trending hashtags. They know how to make their voices heard and can rally behind a cause with passion and creativity.

Meanwhile, **McFly's Galaxy Defenders** have created a vast

network of fan accounts, forums, and social media groups that keep the fandom connected. They're always sharing memes, fan art, and clips of their favorite McFly moments, creating an online presence that's as wholesome as it is devoted.

The Verdict: Who's More Hardcore?

It's a tough call. Both fanbases are **incredibly dedicated**, fiercely loyal, and willing to go the extra mile for their favorite band. **Busted's Army** may have the edge when it comes to **overcoming adversity**—after all, they kept the faith through a decade-long hiatus, proving that their love for the band transcends time. But **McFly's Galaxy Defenders** have shown **consistent dedication** for nearly two decades, never wavering in their support and creating a family-like community that spans the globe.

In the end, there's no real winner or loser here—both fanbases are hardcore in their own right, and it's that passion and love for their bands that have made **Busted and McFly** the pop-rock legends they are today. So whether you're a proud member of **Busted's Army** or one of the loyal **Galaxy Defenders**, one thing's for sure: these fans are here to stay, and they're not backing down any time soon!

8

Memorable Collaborations and Crossover Moments

Busted and McFly may have taken the pop-rock world by storm as individual bands, but when it comes to **collaborations and side projects**, they've gone well beyond their own iconic hits. These two bands have crossed musical boundaries, teamed up with other artists, and even joined forces in the form of **McBusted**—the ultimate **Band vs Band** crossover! But before we dive into that legendary supergroup, let's take a trip through some of the most **memorable collaborations** and side projects involving Busted, focusing on how they've spread their pop-punk wings beyond their own albums.

From **James Bourne's Son of Dork** days to **Charlie Simpson's solo career**, each member of Busted has had their own journey outside of the band, exploring new sounds, styles, and partnerships. And, of course, we can't forget how these side projects have created some unforgettable **crossover moments** that have given fans even more reasons to love these talented musicians.

Busted's Side Projects and Collaborations: A Look at the Boys Beyond the Band

James Bourne: The Pop-Punk Architect

Let's kick things off with **James Bourne**, Busted's **songwriting mastermind**. While James made a name for himself as the cheeky, energetic glue holding Busted together, his talents didn't stop there. In fact, after Busted's initial breakup in 2005, James quickly dove into a new project: the pop-punk band **Son of Dork**. If you loved Busted's signature sound, Son of Dork was like taking it up a notch, with more power chords, witty lyrics, and that signature mix of fun and rebellion.

Son of Dork was James's way of keeping the pop-punk dream alive. Their debut album, **"Welcome to Loserville,"** was packed with catchy, energetic tracks like **"Ticket Outta Loserville"** and **"Eddie's Song,"** which echoed the same infectious, youthful energy that made Busted so popular. But unlike Busted, Son of Dork leaned even further into the **American high-school movie vibe**, with songs that felt like the perfect soundtrack for a teen comedy. Think **"American Pie"** meets **"Skater Boy"**—the perfect combo for anyone who wasn't quite ready to leave the Year 3000 behind.

Even though Son of Dork only lasted for one album, their impact on James's career—and pop-punk fans everywhere—was huge. The band may have been short-lived, but it kept the **Busted sound** alive during the dark years of the band's hiatus. Plus, James's work with Son of Dork solidified his reputation as one of the UK's top pop-punk songwriters, influencing a new generation of bands in the genre.

After Son of Dork, James continued to flex his songwriting muscles, co-writing songs for other artists and dabbling in **musical theater**. He co-wrote songs for acts like **5 Seconds of Summer** and **The Vamps**, showing that his talent for crafting catchy hooks and relatable lyrics was still in high demand. One of his standout achievements? Co-writing **"Loserville: The Musical"**, a stage show based on Son of Dork's album. It was a fun, theatrical twist that proved James could take his pop-punk sensibilities into brand-new territories.

Charlie Simpson: The Indie-Rock Adventurer

If James was the pop-punk prince, **Charlie Simpson** was the band's resident **rock god**, and after leaving Busted, he wasn't about to stick with the same sound. In a move that shocked fans, Charlie left behind the world of **"What I Go to School For"** and dove headfirst into the **indie-rock scene** with his band **Fightstar**.

Fightstar was Charlie's chance to explore a heavier, more emotional sound, rooted in **post-hardcore** and **alternative rock**. Tracks like **"Palahniuk's Laughter"** and **"Grand Unification (Part 1)"** were a far cry from Busted's cheeky pop-punk anthems, showing Charlie's versatility as a musician. His deep, growling vocals and complex guitar work brought an edgier, more mature sound to his new fanbase, while still maintaining some of the energy that had made Busted's music so addictive.

But even though Fightstar was worlds away from the pop-punk

scene, Charlie's transition into indie-rock didn't alienate his old fans—in fact, many Busted fans followed him into this new musical chapter, appreciating his willingness to experiment and push his creative boundaries. Fightstar released several critically acclaimed albums, including **"Grand Unification"** and **"Be Human,"** earning Charlie a whole new set of fans who loved his darker, heavier sound.

And as if that wasn't enough, Charlie also embarked on a **successful solo career**, bringing a more acoustic, singer-songwriter vibe to the table. His solo albums, like **"Young Pilgrim"** and **"Long Road Home,"** showed off his softer, more introspective side, with tracks like **"Parachutes"** and **"Cemetery"** offering heartfelt lyrics and soothing acoustic melodies. It was yet another example of how **musically versatile** Charlie truly is.

Matt Willis: The Reality TV Star-Turned-Rockstar

While **Matt Willis** might have been Busted's resident troublemaker on stage, he found his groove in the world of **reality TV** after the band's breakup. Matt famously competed in and won **"I'm a Celebrity… Get Me Out of Here!"** in 2006, showing that he was more than just a pop-punk bassist—he was also a reality TV star with a serious knack for surviving the Australian jungle.

But don't let his reality TV fame fool you—Matt didn't leave music behind. He released his own solo album, **"Don't Let It Go to Waste,"** which brought a more pop-rock sound to his repertoire. Tracks like **"Up All Night"** and **"Hey Kid"** showcased Matt's ability to hold his own as a solo artist, and his charming, rebellious personality shone through in his music videos and performances.

In addition to his solo work, Matt continued to collaborate with other artists and even reunited with James Bourne for a short-lived project called **"Bourne & Willis."** Though it didn't take off in the same way as their previous work, it was a fun reminder of their shared musical chemistry.

Busted's Big Crossover Moment: The Rise of McBusted

We can't talk about **Busted's collaborations** without mentioning the **ultimate crossover moment**: **McBusted**. When **Busted and McFly** joined forces in 2014 to form the **supergroup** we never knew we needed, it was like a pop-rock dream come true. Fans of both bands had speculated for years about what might happen if the two iconic groups teamed up, and McBusted proved that the result was even better than expected.

The collaboration came about when James, Matt, and McFly's members reunited for a few **live performances**. The chemistry between the two bands was undeniable, and soon enough, McBusted was born. Their joint tour was a massive success, with fans across the UK flocking to arenas to see their favorite hits from both bands performed in one epic show.

McFly's Side Projects and Collaborations: The Era of McBusted and Beyond

When it comes to **side projects and collaborations**, **McFly** has never been content to stick to just one lane. Whether teaming up with fellow pop-rock legends **Busted** to form the ultimate supergroup, exploring solo ventures, or lending their songwriting talents to other artists, McFly has continuously evolved and expanded their musical horizons. The most iconic of these collaborations, of course, is the **McBusted** era—a fan-fueled fusion that took both bands to new heights and set the stage for the upcoming **Band vs Band** world tour.

In this chapter, we're diving into the **McBusted phenomenon**, exploring how this unlikely supergroup came together, the hits they created, and the unforgettable tour that had fans screaming in arenas across the UK. But first, let's take a look at the individual side projects and collaborations that helped McFly's members grow as artists outside of their core band.

McFly's Side Projects: Exploring New Frontiers

Tom Fletcher: The Multitalented Hitmaker

When it comes to **songwriting**, **Tom Fletcher** is an absolute powerhouse. While he's best known for penning McFly's biggest hits, Tom's talents extend well beyond his own band. In fact, he's written songs for some of the **biggest names in pop**, including **One Direction**, for whom he co-wrote the chart-topping single **"I Want"**. His ability to craft catchy, memorable tunes has made him one of the most sought-after songwriters in the business, and his writing credits span across numerous pop hits.

But Tom isn't just a songwriter—he's also a successful **author**. His children's books, including **"The Dinosaur That Pooped"** series and **"The Christmasaurus,"** have become bestsellers, showcasing his creativity in a completely different arena. The whimsical stories and charming characters in his books mirror the playful energy of his music, proving that Tom's imagination knows no bounds.

Danny Jones: Rock and Soul Experimentation

Danny Jones has always been the rock 'n' roll heart of McFly, bringing his bluesy guitar riffs and soulful voice to the band's biggest hits. But when he's not rocking out with McFly, Danny has explored his love of **DJing and electronic music**. In his side project as a DJ, Danny remixed tracks and played sets that combined his rock sensibilities with electronic beats, showing off his versatility as a musician.

In addition to his solo music, Danny has appeared as a **coach on "The Voice Kids UK"**, where he's helped mentor the next generation of singers. His experience as both a performer and a songwriter has made him an invaluable mentor, and his infectious enthusiasm for music shines through in his work with young artists.

Dougie Poynter: Punk, Fashion, and the Jungle

Dougie Poynter, McFly's quirky and loveable bassist, has had quite the **eclectic career**. After McFly's initial rise to fame, Dougie dipped his toes into the world of **punk music** with his side project **INK.**, a band that showcased a darker, more alternative sound compared to McFly's upbeat pop-rock. His punk influence, paired with his offbeat style, brought a new dimension to his musical identity.

But music isn't Dougie's only passion—he's also a **fashion icon** and an **author**. Dougie has modeled for major fashion brands and co-written a children's book, **"Plastic Sucks!"**, which focuses on raising awareness about environmental issues. And let's not forget his stint on **"I'm a Celebrity... Get Me Out of Here!"**, where he won the hearts of viewers and emerged as the 2011 champion.

Harry Judd: Rhythms, Writing, and Fitness

As McFly's drummer, **Harry Judd** has always kept the beat steady, but his talents extend far beyond the drum kit. Harry's rhythm isn't just reserved for music—he's also a **champion dancer**, having won **"Strictly Come Dancing"** in 2011. His smooth moves and undeniable charisma helped him take home the coveted glitterball trophy, proving that he's as skilled on the dance floor as he is behind the drum set.

Harry has also ventured into the world of **writing and fitness**, publishing his book **"Get Fit, Get Happy"**, which blends his personal experiences with fitness advice, helping fans lead healthier, happier lives. His journey from drummer to fitness guru shows how multifaceted McFly's members really are, both in music and beyond.

McBusted: The Ultimate Fusion of Pop-Rock Greatness

Now, let's get to the heart of one of the most iconic moments in UK pop-rock history: the formation of **McBusted**. What started as a few casual performances between **McFly** and members of **Busted** turned into a **supergroup sensation** that took fans by storm and reminded the world just how fun pop-punk could be.

The Birth of McBusted

In 2013, when **James Bourne** and **Matt Willis** from **Busted** joined McFly on stage for a few surprise performances, the chemistry between the two bands was undeniable. Fans had long speculated about what might happen if Busted and McFly ever joined forces, and the energy from those early performances was electric. The demand for more was immediate and intense, and thus, **McBusted** was born.

What made McBusted so exciting wasn't just the combination of two beloved bands—it was the way they brought together the best of both worlds. They didn't just perform each other's hits; they **created new music together** and embarked on a massive tour that brought nostalgia and fresh energy in equal measure.

Key Songs and Hits from McBusted

McBusted wasn't just about reliving past glories—although fans certainly got plenty of **"Year 3000"** and **"All About You"** moments. The supergroup also wrote and released original songs, including the single **"Air Guitar,"** which became an instant fan favorite. The song was a perfect mix of Busted's cheeky pop-punk attitude and McFly's polished, feel-good sound. Lyrics like **"I don't need no money, I don't need no car / I just want to rock on my air guitar"** captured the playful spirit of McBusted, blending humor with infectious energy.

The release of their self-titled album, **"McBusted"**, included other standout tracks like **"Hate Your Guts"** and **"What Happened to Your Band?"**—a song that reflected on the breakup of Busted and the journey that led them to McBusted. The fusion of both bands' styles created a unique sound that felt fresh while still honoring the legacy of each group's music.

The McBusted Tour: A Pop-Rock Extravaganza

McBusted's **2014 tour** was nothing short of a **pop-rock extravaganza**. Fans flocked to arenas across the UK, thrilled to see the ultimate mash-up of their favorite bands. The setlists were packed with the biggest hits from both bands, giving fans the best of Busted and McFly in one epic concert. From **"Crashed the Wedding"** to **"Five Colours in Her Hair,"** the shows were a celebration of everything that made these bands iconic.

The **stage production** was just as wild and fun as the music itself. With giant props (like a spaceship!) and hilarious skits between songs, McBusted's live performances were more than just concerts—they were full-blown **theatrical events** that had fans dancing, laughing, and screaming for more.

Fan Reaction and Impact

The response to McBusted was overwhelming. For many fans, it felt like the ultimate pop-punk dream come true—a once-in-a-lifetime fusion of their two favorite bands. The nostalgia factor was high, but it wasn't just about looking back. McBusted's new music and larger-than-life shows breathed new life into both bands' legacies, attracting a new generation of fans while keeping their original fanbases engaged.

This successful collaboration not only reignited the careers of both Busted and McFly, but it also laid the groundwork for the **upcoming Band vs Band tour**. McBusted proved that there was still **massive fan demand** for these bands, and the idea of bringing them back together—this time in friendly competition—was a natural next step.

How McBusted Set the Stage for the Band vs Band Tour

McBusted wasn't just a nostalgic blast from the past; it was a **game-changer** for both bands. The supergroup reminded everyone just how powerful the pop-punk and pop-rock combo could be, and it opened the door for even bigger things down the line. The success of McBusted showed that **Busted and McFly's fanbases were as loyal as ever**, and the incredible chemistry between the two bands was undeniable.

Now, with the **Band vs Band tour**, fans are getting the best of both worlds once again—this time with a competitive twist. The tour promises to reignite the friendly rivalry between Busted and McFly, allowing each band to show off their unique strengths while celebrating the shared musical legacy they've built over the years.

As we gear up for the **ultimate showdown**, it's clear that McBusted was more than just a one-off project—it was the perfect prelude to the epic **Busted vs McFly battle** that's about to take the stage. Buckle up, because this **crossover moment** is about to go down in **pop-rock history**!

9

Behind the Scenes: Fun Facts, Trivia, and Easter Eggs

Ready to dive deeper into the **Busted vs McFly** universe? If you think you know everything there is to know about these two pop-rock powerhouses, buckle up because we're about to uncover some hidden gems, quirky trivia, and Easter eggs that will take your fandom to the next level. Whether you're a hardcore member of **Busted's Army** or a loyal **Galaxy Defender**, this chapter is packed with insider info, behind-the-scenes stories, and fun facts that you might have missed. Get ready to explore the world of **Busted** and **McFly** like never before!

Busted Trivia: Secrets from the Year 3000 and Beyond

Busted might have been singing about crashing weddings and time travel, but there's a lot more going on behind the scenes of their music than meets the eye. From hidden details in their music videos to the **meaning behind their lyrics**, here are some fun facts about Busted that even the most die-hard fans might not know.

Hidden Details in Music Videos

- **"Year 3000"** – Let's start with the iconic **"Year 3000"** music video. Did you know that the **futuristic underwater city** the band visits is actually a nod to their obsession with science fiction? James Bourne, the band's resident sci-fi fan, helped infuse the video with playful references to **Back to the Future**, as well as his favorite space-themed TV shows. Keep an eye out for the hovering guitars in the video, a cheeky nod to the idea that Busted's music is still relevant 1,000 years into the future (and let's be honest, it probably will be!).

- **"What I Go to School For"** – The inspiration behind this cheeky song came from a real-life crush of **James Bourne**! In fact, James has admitted that the song is based on his high school days when he had a crush on one of his teachers (we're looking at you, Miss Mackenzie!). The music video features the boys sneaking around their school in a series of rebellious pranks, but keep an eye out for the **subtle nods to their own school experiences**—from messy lockers to daydreams of the Year 3000.

- **"Crashed the Wedding"** – If you've ever watched this

music video and thought, "That looks like one of the most chaotic weddings ever," you're not wrong! But did you know that some of the **extras in the video** were real fans of the band? Busted invited a handful of fans to be part of the raucous wedding crash, making this video an even more fan-centered experience.

Fun Facts About Their Lyrics and Albums

- **"Sleeping with the Light On"** – This emotional ballad might sound like a simple breakup song, but according to **Matt Willis**, it's actually based on a very specific incident where he found himself in an incredibly awkward post-breakup moment. He once explained that it was about "feeling lonely but still wanting someone to call even when you know it's over."

- **Charlie's Solo on "3AM"** – Busted's hit **"3AM"** is known for its heart-wrenching lyrics, but what fans might not know is that **Charlie Simpson** actually fought hard to have a **guitar solo** included in the song. It was one of the first times that Charlie really got to showcase his **heavier rock influences** in a Busted track, foreshadowing his transition into the world of post-hardcore with Fightstar.

Inside Jokes and Band Secrets

- Busted has a number of inside jokes that have made their way into their lyrics. In the song **"Dawson's Geek,"** the lyrics poke fun at **James Bourne's** obsession with the TV show **Dawson's Creek**. James was a massive fan of the show and often joked about how it captured all of his teenage drama feelings, so naturally, he worked it into a song!
- Did you know that Busted has an **unofficial mascot**? During their early years, they carried around a **stuffed penguin** named Percy on tour with them, claiming that Percy was their "tour good luck charm." Fans who followed the band closely during their early tours might remember spotting Percy in backstage photos.

McFly Trivia: Backstage Shenanigans and Hidden References

McFly's rise to fame has been filled with laughter, mischief, and plenty of **behind-the-scenes stories** that show just how much fun this band has together. From on-stage pranks to tour bus antics, here are some of the most amusing and surprising facts about McFly's adventures.

Stories from Their Tours

- **The "Wonderland Tour" Pillow Fights** – During McFly's **Wonderland Tour**, the band became notorious for their backstage pillow fights. It all started as a joke between **Dougie Poynter** and **Danny Jones**, but before long, every tour stop turned into a full-on battle with pillows flying

around backstage. Fans who waited outside venues often saw feathers spilling out of dressing rooms after the band's infamous pillow wars!
- **The Band's Fake Names** – McFly has always had a playful side, and one of their favorite pranks during tours was checking into hotels under **ridiculous fake names**. **Harry Judd** once revealed that they used names like **"Elvis McFly"** or **"The Super Duper Band"** when booking hotel rooms just to make their team and the hotel staff laugh.
- **Tom's Marriage Proposal** – One of the sweetest McFly fan moments happened when **Tom Fletcher** proposed to his girlfriend, **Giovanna**, in a music video-style montage featuring all of their memories together. Tom wrote a song for the proposal and then later incorporated parts of that song into McFly's live shows, creating an unforgettable moment for fans who had followed the couple's story.

Hidden References in Songs

- **"Star Girl"** – McFly's hit **"Star Girl"** is more than just a fun, upbeat track; it's packed with hidden meanings and Easter eggs. For example, the "sending a message to the moon" lyric was inspired by a joke the band had about trying to **reach space** with their music. They even had fans "send messages to the moon" by texting in their support during live shows!

- **The Heart Never Lies"** – In this heartfelt ballad, McFly addresses their own journey as a band and the highs and lows they've experienced together. But there's a hidden reference in the song—one of the lines, **"Another year over, and we're still together,"** was a personal nod to the challenges they faced after their first few years in the music industry. The song became a fan favorite because of its deeply personal connection to the band's real-life struggles and successes.

Amusing Behind-the-Scenes Moments

- During the recording of their **"Motion in the Ocean"** album, McFly spent days pulling pranks on each other in the studio. One of the most legendary moments involved **Dougie Poynter** filling **Tom Fletcher's** recording booth with balloons, leaving Tom stuck in a sea of colorful orbs while trying to record his vocals. The band later shared footage of the prank, and it became a fan favorite moment in their behind-the-scenes content.

Easter Eggs for Hardcore Fans: Connecting the Dots Between Busted and McFly

If you've been following **Busted** and **McFly** for years, you've probably noticed some subtle (and not-so-subtle) **overlapping themes** in their music, lyrics, and even the way they've referenced each other over the years. Here are a few Easter eggs that only the most **hardcore fans** would catch:

BEHIND THE SCENES: FUN FACTS, TRIVIA, AND EASTER EGGS

- **James Bourne and Tom Fletcher**: These two have been **songwriting buddies** for years, and their collaborations go back long before **McBusted**. The pair actually wrote songs for each other's bands early in their careers. One of the most famous crossovers is **"Five Colours in Her Hair,"** McFly's debut single, which was co-written by James. The song's playful, pop-punk vibe was a perfect match for both bands' sounds.
- **The Year 3000 Connection**: McFly has performed Busted's iconic track **"Year 3000"** live during numerous shows, even before the formation of McBusted. Fans loved the way McFly added their own twist to the song, and it became an ongoing joke that McFly could "travel through time" in their songs too, thanks to their 2006 hit **"Transylvania"**.
- **Dougie's Dinosaur Obsession**: Dougie Poynter, as many fans know, is obsessed with dinosaurs. His love for prehistoric creatures pops up in interviews, social media posts, and even on stage. Busted's reunion album **"Night Driver"** features a track called **"Kids with Computers,"** which Dougie jokingly claimed was inspired by his imaginary dinosaur friends (don't worry, Dougie—dinosaurs will always have a place in our hearts too).

Final Thoughts: The Ultimate Fan Easter Egg Hunt

From backstage antics to secret nods between bands, both **Busted** and **McFly** have left a trail of **Easter eggs and fun facts** for their most dedicated fans to uncover. Whether it's hidden details in music videos, stories from their tours, or the moments when the two bands' worlds collide, there's always something new to discover for those who are paying attention.

As we gear up for the **Band vs Band** tour, we can't wait to see what new **behind-the-scenes stories** and inside jokes come to life on stage. Keep your eyes peeled—you never know what hidden gems these bands will sneak into their performances next!

10

The Verdict: Who Reigns Supreme?

The stage is set, the battle lines have been drawn, and the amps have been cranked up to 11. After a deep dive into **Busted** and **McFly**'s music, live performances, chart success, fashion statements, and fanbase rivalries, it's time for the ultimate showdown: **Who reigns supreme?**

It's not an easy decision. Both bands have built massive fanbases, crafted hit after hit, and left their mark on the pop-rock landscape in ways that are impossible to ignore. So, let's go category by category, comparing **Busted's punk-pop rebellion** with **McFly's polished pop-rock charm**, and figure out which band truly comes out on top in this **Band vs Band** battle. Ready to settle the score? Let's dive in!

Music: Punk-Pop Hits vs. Pop-Rock Perfection

Busted burst onto the scene with songs that were fast, cheeky, and full of **youthful rebellion**. Tracks like **"Year 3000," "What I Go to School For,"** and **"Crashed the Wedding"** became instant anthems for anyone who ever felt like causing a little chaos. With their signature power chords, witty lyrics, and relentless energy, Busted cemented themselves as pop-punk royalty. Their influence even extended to the next generation of pop-punk bands, including **5 Seconds of Summer** and **The Vamps**, showing just how enduring their sound has been.

On the other hand, **McFly** brought a sunnier, more polished sound to the mix. Their debut single, **"Five Colours in Her Hair,"** made it clear that McFly was all about catchy, feel-good pop-rock. Their knack for crafting infectious melodies and heartfelt lyrics—like in **"All About You"** and **"Obviously"**—gave McFly a broader appeal, making them a staple for fans who wanted both fun and emotional depth. Add in their harmonies, their clever arrangements, and their ability to swing from upbeat bops to tear-jerking ballads, and it's clear why McFly has remained such a pop-rock powerhouse.

Verdict:

When it comes to **sheer energy and rebellion**, **Busted** takes the crown with their pop-punk anthems. But if we're talking about **musical versatility and polished perfection**, **McFly** pulls ahead. It's a close call, but we'll call this one a **draw**, because let's face it: both bands have mastered their respective sounds!

Live Performances: Chaotic Fun vs. Polished Showmanship

When **Busted** hits the stage, it's like a controlled explosion of **punk-pop chaos**. From the moment they launch into their high-energy hits, it's a wild ride of jumping, shredding guitars, and sing-along anthems that have fans on their feet from start to finish. Busted is known for their unpredictability on stage—whether it's **Matt Willis** stage-diving into the crowd or **James Bourne** cracking jokes mid-set, there's always a sense that anything could happen. Their live shows feel like a punk-pop party, full of spontaneity and pure fun.

McFly, on the other hand, brings a different kind of energy to the stage. Their performances are tight, well-rehearsed, and packed with **musical precision**. While Busted thrives on chaos, McFly excels in crafting a seamless live experience that balances humor, charm, and emotional depth. **Tom, Danny, Dougie, and Harry** know how to work a crowd, often engaging in banter, pulling off surprise covers, and inviting fans to be part of the show. Whether they're rocking out to **"Star Girl"** or slowing things down with **"The Heart Never Lies,"** McFly's performances are full of feel-good vibes and heartfelt moments.

Verdict:

If you're looking for a **wild, unpredictable party**, Busted's live shows are hard to beat. But if you want a more **polished, emotionally engaging performance**, McFly has the edge. Once again, it's a matter of taste—but for overall **stagecraft and crowd interaction**, McFly takes this round.

Chart Success: Who Ruled the Airwaves?

When it comes to **chart success**, both Busted and McFly have had their moments of glory. **Busted** scored hit after hit during their early years, racking up **four UK #1 singles**, including **"Crashed the Wedding"** and **"Who's David?"** Their albums consistently hit the top of the charts, with their debut album reaching **#2** and their follow-up album, **"A Present for Everyone,"** dominating the charts as well. Though their run was shorter due to their initial breakup, Busted's chart dominance was intense while it lasted.

Meanwhile, **McFly** has an impressive record of **seven UK #1 singles** and **two UK #1 albums**. Their debut album, **"Room on the 3rd Floor,"** made them the youngest band ever to have an album debut at #1, a record they still hold. Hits like **"All About You," "Obviously,"** and **"Please, Please"** helped them maintain a consistent presence at the top of the charts. And with **18 UK Top 10 singles**, McFly's success on the charts speaks for itself.

Verdict:

When it comes to **chart-topping singles and albums**, **McFly** reigns supreme. Their consistent presence in the charts, combined with their record-breaking debut, gives them the win in this category.

Style Showdown: Grunge-Pop vs. Surfer-Chic

Fashion isn't just about clothes—it's about **attitude**, and both Busted and McFly have had their own iconic looks over the years. **Busted's style** was all about **grunge-pop rebellion**. From their ripped jeans and Converse sneakers to their scruffy hair and punk accessories, Busted's early look was the embodiment of 2000s punk-pop cool. Their fashion sense mirrored their music: fun, irreverent, and a little rough around the edges.

McFly, on the other hand, embraced a more **preppy, surfer-chic vibe**. With their striped polo shirts, Converse sneakers, and sun-kissed hair, McFly looked like they'd just stepped off a beach in California. Their fashion sense evolved over the years, moving from **boyish charm** to a more polished rock-star look as they matured. Whether they were rocking leather jackets or cardigans, McFly always had a clean, fresh look that contrasted with Busted's grunge aesthetic.

Verdict:

If you're into **grunge and rebellion**, Busted's early style will be your favorite. But for those who prefer a **clean-cut, preppy look**, McFly takes the crown. It's another close call, but McFly's **fashion evolution** gives them a slight edge in this category.

Fanbase: Busted's Army vs. McFly's Galaxy Defenders

Let's not forget the **true heroes** of this rivalry: the fans. **Busted's Army** has been through it all, from the band's early days to their heartbreaking breakup and eventual reunion. Their dedication never wavered, and they fought hard to bring Busted back after their hiatus, launching social media campaigns and petitions to make their voices heard. Their loyalty is fierce, and they've been there for every chaotic live show and every new album.

McFly's Galaxy Defenders, on the other hand, have shown unwavering support since day one. Their fanbase is known for being one of the most **loyal, passionate groups** in pop-rock, creating fan projects, trending hashtags, and supporting the band through every evolution of their sound. McFly's deep connection with their fans has always been a hallmark of their career, from their **SuperCity platform** to their fan-driven setlists.

Verdict:

Both fanbases are **hardcore** in their own right, but for their **sheer dedication and engagement**, **McFly's Galaxy Defenders** take the win in this category. Their connection with the band is legendary, and they've played a major role in McFly's continued success.

THE VERDICT: WHO REIGNS SUPREME?

Audience Interaction: Time to Vote!

Now it's your turn to **cast your vote** and help decide who reigns supreme in the **Band vs Band** showdown. Are you team **Busted**, the kings of pop-punk chaos, or team **McFly**, the masters of feel-good pop-rock? Here are a few questions to help you make your decision:

- **Which band left a bigger impact on pop culture?** Did Busted's cheeky anthems shape your teenage years, or did McFly's heartfelt ballads hit you right in the feels?
- **Who delivers the better live show?** Do you crave the chaotic energy of a Busted gig, or do you prefer McFly's polished, crowd-pleasing performances?
- **Whose songs are still stuck in your head?** Whether you're still singing **"Year 3000"** or belting out **"All About You,"** it's time to decide who created the ultimate soundtrack to your life.

The Ultimate Showdown

At the end of the day, the **Busted vs McFly** battle isn't just about who's better—it's about celebrating two bands that have defined the **pop-rock landscape** for nearly two decades. Whether you're loyal to the **punk-pop rebellion** of Busted or the **feel-good charm** of McFly, one thing is clear: both bands have left an indelible mark on music history.

So, cast your vote, rock out to your favorite tracks, and get ready for the **ultimate showdown** when these two bands hit the stage together for the **Band vs Band** tour. Let the battle begin!

11

A Legacy of Two Legendary Bands

As the amps are turned down and the final notes of **"Year 3000"** and **"Five Colours in Her Hair"** fade into the night, one thing is abundantly clear: **Busted** and **McFly** are more than just bands—they're **icons** of an era, legends of the pop-rock world. From their earliest days of cheeky lyrics and catchy riffs to their massive world tours and collaborative supergroup **McBusted**, both bands have made an unforgettable impact on the music industry. As they gear up for the epic **Band vs Band** tour, we find ourselves asking, "What's next for these two musical giants?"

In this conclusion, we'll explore the significance of this joint world tour, the lasting influence that **Busted** and **McFly** have had on the music scene, and what the future might hold for both bands. Buckle up, because even though the tour might be the final showdown, this is far from the end of the road for either band. **The heart never lies**, after all!

Looking Ahead: The Significance of the Band vs Band World Tour

The **Band vs Band** world tour isn't just another series of concerts—it's a monumental moment in both bands' histories. For **Busted** and **McFly**, it's an opportunity to celebrate their individual legacies while giving fans the ultimate gift: a once-in-a-lifetime chance to see these two bands battle it out on stage in a friendly, fan-fueled competition. This tour marks the culmination of years of growth, evolution, and a lot of **"Star Girl"**-level excitement.

But this isn't just about looking back at the good old days. The **Band vs Band** tour represents a new chapter for both bands, proving that they are still relevant, still beloved, and still capable of delivering a jaw-dropping live experience. It's not just a nostalgia trip—it's a **celebration of longevity**. With each band bringing their A-game to the stage, the tour shows that both Busted and McFly have more than earned their place in the pop-rock pantheon. It's not just about winning the competition, it's about **rocking the world together**.

For the fans, this tour is a dream come true. Whether you're rooting for Busted's punk-pop anthems or McFly's feel-good harmonies, there's no doubt that this tour is the ultimate fan-service event. And for the bands, it's a chance to reconnect with their audiences on a grand scale, to bring back the hits that defined a generation, and to celebrate the **music that made them who they are**. So, as we look ahead, we can be sure of one thing: this tour is a reminder that both Busted and McFly still have plenty of life in them—and they're ready to show the world.

Printed in Great Britain
by Amazon